Chief Justice John Roberts

Traitor or Patriot - You decide!

NEW VIDEO ... "TRAITOR OR PATRIOT" By TLGA. When the law is there and the statute can be read, why is America *NOT BOTHERING TO LOOK!* and instead has decided that this man is a traitor?

Do you have any idea what he has done for us? The ONLY thing he *COULD* do for us? *SETTING IT UP FOR US TO ENFORCE.*

Listen to and watch this video *CAREFULLY! THEN CELEBRATE !!! THEN COME TOGETHER IN NON-COMPLIANCE !!!*

TRAITOR OR PATRIOT
http://youtu.be/9kMxC5HYnGY

Why do people take the Government Media's word for anything? Why are people not able to simply read a court ruling, look up the cited statutes and codes and discern for themselves for themselves what the court ruling really means? Wake up America and do it. This ruling is not what you have been falsely led to believe it is.

Video Transcript

Good Morning Congress! It's us again; The People; Seeing Something and (Yup) Saying Something. This time the message is delivered specifically to all of us out here who don't know just yet what is really going on and why *YOU PEOPLE IN CONGRESS* don't want us to know.

But in the interest of fair-play we share the message with you too. We're coming for you. Each and every one of you when next you have the audacity to attempt to lie to us, cover your sorry butts and convince us to vote for you.

Some of you may be able to fool some of the people some of the time, but you will *never* fool any of the people all of the time — *and you're time is up!*

The following Article was sent to me (TLGA) via email this morning, and thank you Keith for sending it. I agree with him that every American needs to make his or her own choices and form his or her own actions in regard to the BS fakery known as *Obamacare.*

But no one should make any decision until reading this Article very carefully or listening to it over and over again since part of *the Plan* to bring this nation down was and is the complete dumbing down of the populace; and heavy indoctrination, instead of education in our schools.

Too many of us cannot read, will not read, or simply do not have the time to read because they are working 2 or 3 jobs just to feed themselves. So for those who prefer audio, I'll read the Article and then I'll send it out in text, far and wide.

You should all, certainly do what you want, but Keith and I highly suggest that you *do not sign up for Obamacare* until you read or listen to this; carefully.

Chief Justice Roberts carefully worded his ruling, and did not include any _requirement to participate_ for 95% of Americans!

One Stone, Two Powers: How Chief Justice Roberts Saved America

Original Author Unknown

"So David triumphed over the Philistine with a sling and a stone; without a sword in his hand, he struck down the Philistine and killed him." — *1 Samuel 17:50.*

Many people are very angry at Chief Justice John Roberts for his ruling that *"Obamacare is Constitutional as a tax"*. They are outraged at what they see as his validation of _the complete usurpation_ of Constitutional protections and terrified that America has been effectively destroyed. Some of them are even talking *"revolution,"* and asking each other in person, and in print, *"what are you prepared to do"*?

Well this analysis of the Roberts ruling asks the same thing but in a different context. What _are_ you prepared to do? Are you, for example, prepared to read? Are you prepared to learn? Are you prepared to entertain the concept that you might be wrong about Roberts – about what he actually ruled, about what he actually meant, about what he actually did, and why the rest of the Court would not stand with him?

Because if you aren't, then don't bother reading any further. Beware: *this analysis pops bubbles* - *hard*. Here's a taste of what I mean:

You know all the yowling and screaming about how Roberts *changed a penalty into a tax*? In his ruling Roberts quoted *Obamacar,* itself, **Title 26, §5000A(g)(1)** which reads:

The penalty provided by this section...shall be assessed and collected in the same manner as an assessable penalty under **subchapter B of chapter 68**.

Then Roberts did this *amazing totally judicial thing* that no one else can possibly do except someone with his vast power at their fingertips – *he actually looked up the law that Obamacare quoted.* And when he did, he found that **subchapter B of chapter 68**, specifically at **§6671(a)**, says:

The penalties and liabilities provided by this subchapter shall be...assessed and collected in the same manner as taxes. ...any reference in this title to "tax" imposed by this title shall be deemed also to refer to the penalties and liabilities provided by this subchapter.

Then after reading these actual laws cited by Obamacare itself, Roberts made this blockbuster observation: *"The requirement to pay is found in the Internal Revenue Code and enforced by the IRS, which, as we previously explained, must* <u>*assess and collect*</u> *it in the same manner as taxes."*

Let's see; Roberts said the penalty must be assessed and collected *"in the same manner as taxes"* after reading that *Obamacare itself invokes §6671(a),* which literally and specifically states that the penalty must be assessed and collected *"in the same manner as taxes."*

Wow, that's a radical ruling.

And what exactly is *§6671(a)*? It's a part of the Internal Revenue Code *that was there before Obamacare was even created!* All *Obamacare* did was point to it and say *"use that".*

So why weren't Americans enraged about how *§6671(a)* equated the treatment of penalties as taxes *before Obamacare?*

People can disagree with him if they want to but how the hell can anyone say **"Roberts is legislating from the bench"** when he simply *repeats pre-existing tax law* that *Obamacare references for itself?* Of course, *the answer to that question is simple* — no one actually *looked up the laws* before they decided that their country has been *"destroyed."* Yet they're ready to fight a bloody **"revolution"** over it!

A revolution for *what*—to make new laws that they *still* won't read?

If you want to get angry, get angry about how *the other eight Justices didn't point out this simple fact* about penalties *already* being treated as taxes. After all, that's what judges are supposed to do. Right? Point out <u>what the law is</u>, *rather than what anyone wants* it to be? *Right?*

And isn't that exactly what Chief Justice Roberts did here?

Maybe that's why he's Chief Justice — *he gets to read the actual laws.* Maybe all the other Justices have to *listen to the media* to find out how they should rule.

So you're warned: *This analysis is not for the squeamish.* But if you *really* want to learn what Roberts did, *and why he did it,* and *what* the *Obamacare* tax laws *actually mean* (as opposed to what you mistakenly *thought* they meant), read on.

And you can start by understanding this:

• Chief Justice Roberts limited the Constitutionality of Obamacare *to ONLY those statutorily-defined "persons" upon whom the income tax is imposed.*

• 95% of the American population are *NOT those statutorily-defined "persons".*

• **Therefore: Obamacare *does NOT* apply to 95% of the American population!**

Don't believe me? Then, like I said, read on . . .

Point #1: *Imposed means Enforced –* (Part 1)

Taxes—*whether voluntary or not*—are subject to *enforcement*. If a tax can't be enforced it's not a tax.

That's why the income tax law **Title 26, Chapter 1, Section 1** starts out with: *"There is hereby imposed on the taxable income of every individual…"*

And the *Obamacare* law, **Title 26, § 5000 A(b)(1)** starts

6

out with: *"There is hereby imposed on the taxpayer who is an applicable individual a penalty..."*

Notice the mutual use of the word _imposed_? It means _enforced_ by the government.

Point #2: *Obamacare* is part of the Income Tax Laws

Obamacare, at **Title 26, §5000A(b)(2)** states: *"Any penalty imposed by this section ... shall be included with a taxpayer's return under Chapter 1..."*

Chapter 1 of Title 26 (the Internal Revenue Code) is where the income tax is imposed. **Title 26** is also where *Obamacare* is found. So when *Obamacare* penalties (which enable it to be imposed and therefore enforced) are specified within *Obamacare* itself to be *part of the income tax return,* they are *also* thereby making those penalties subject to the income tax enforcement laws of **Title 26**.

Point #3: Obamacare is Written to Deceive

In his ruling, Roberts observed that *Obamacare* specified that its penalty *"shall be assessed and collected in the same manner as an assessable penalty under **subchapter B of chapter 68**"* which in turn specifies that those penalties *"shall be assessed and collected in the same manner as taxes."* Then he notes that the authority for those acts are found in *"**§6201** (assessment authority); **§6301** (collection authority)"* which are the same authorities used for _assessing and collecting_ income taxes.

Then Roberts says something very curious. He says that *"interpretation is consistent with the remainder of §5000A(g) which instructs the Secretary on the tools he may use to collect the penalty. See §5000A(g)(2)(A) - barring criminal prosecutions - and §5000A(g)(2)(B) - prohibiting the Secretary from using notices of lien and levies."*

Look what stands out – what Roberts is saying is that *"tools that may be <u>used</u> to collect the penalty"* are actually - if you look at his parenthetical descriptions - *denials of the tools <u>necessary</u> to collect the penalty.* The first refers to *"barring criminal prosecutions"* and the second refers to *"prohibiting the Secretary from using notices of lien and levies."*

So how are they *"tools that may be used to collect the penalty"*? And besides, just how is the *Obamacare* tax penalty going to be collected if <u>both</u> *criminal prosecutions* and *liens and levies* cannot be used to go get it?

Roberts is drawing our attention to these statutes. Let's look at them.

Title 26, §5000A(g)(2) says: *Notwithstanding any other provision of law —*

(A) In the case of any failure by a taxpayer to timely pay any penalty imposed by this section, such taxpayer shall not be subject to any criminal prosecution or penalty with respect to such failure.

(B) The Secretary shall not *(i)* file notice of lien with respect to any property of a taxpayer by reason of any

failure to pay the penalty imposed by this section, or **(ii)** levy on any such property with respect to such failure.

Section (A) has to do with "barring criminal prosecutions." Sounds nice, but what does it apply to? It applies to *failure to "timely pay" a penalty.*

Guess what? *Failure to timely pay a penalty* is NOT a criminal act. Usually it invokes further penalties and interest. Only if you *fail to pay altogether* could the situation reach criminal status, and even then, it would have to be *willful.* Otherwise the penalties and interest would just continue to pile up. *"Willful failure to pay"* is *not "failure to timely pay."* So since the ONLY *criminal charge* that *§5000A(g)(2)(A)* protects a taxpayer from *doesn't exist,* the entire statute is a fraud. It's meant to make people think that *Obamacare* is harmless, and that deliberately putting off paying its penalty won't make anyone subject to criminal charges. *But this is not true.*

How about **Section (B)**? Well, *a levy is a seizure of property.* For that to happen, a *lien* has to be filed first specifying what property is to be seized, and that due process has been followed. After the *lien has been filed* but before the *levy is made* upon the property, a *notice of lien* is sent to the taxpayer who owns the property that the government intends to *seize through levy,* to let them know that the *lien has been filed* against them.

Now what does **(B)(i)** say? That a *"notice of lien"* shall *not be filed.* Well, *"notices of lien" aren't filed,* except as copies of the mailing that was made to the taxpayer. *Liens* are filed — *that's* the functional act, *not "notices of lien."*

Filing a *"notice of lien"* is NOT the same thing as filing a *"lien,"* because it *does NOT legally enable a levy.* It's literally just a *"notice"* that an *actual "lien"* has been filed. And it's supposed to be *mailed,* not *"filed."* So when **(B)(i)** forbids it to be filed, well and good, because it's not supposed to be filed anyway! Yet this was obviously written to make you to *think* it's talking about actual *liens,* when it says *"notices of lien"* — when it's not an actual lien.

How about **(B)(ii)**, where it is specified that *no "levy on any such property" shall be made. Well, what "such" property?* The property in **(B)(i)** of course, that was specified in the *"notice of lien".* But wait a second — you can't legally *levy property* from just a *"notice of lien"*! You need a *real* lien to levy property! So this section, once again, is saying that something *illegal* will not be done by the government — specifically, that *no property will seized with only a "notice of lien"* to back up the *levy.* Hey, thanks a *lot.*

So what are we left with here? What did Roberts draw our attention to when he specified laws in *Obamacare* that he said are tools to *collect the penalty,* when they seemed to be tools *to prevent the collection* of the penalty? He did nothing less than to indicate that *these prevention tools are no such thing* — that they block nothing, and that the only actual tools that are indicated, *enable* the *full collection powers* of **Title 26** tax laws to *be used* (i.e., *it's a fully functional Death Star*). And not just those directed by **"subchapter B of chapter 68"**, but *also* criminal penalties, *and lien and levy powers.* Even worse, both of these were cited by *Obamacare* not *only* *to mislead* the public, *but to establish a judicially noticeable reference to legitimize their usage against the public.*

Roberts deliberately drew attention to this. And in doing so, he effectively warned, *"watch out — read carefully, this ruling is dealing with a law that was written to deceive. You have to be very careful in your reading of both it and my ruling if you want to understand what everything really means."*

Then, concerning enforcement, he showed that *nothing in Obamacare blocks the usage of **subchapter B of Chapter 68**, Criminal, or Lien & Levy powers against taxpayers to collect Obamacare penalties.* And most importantly he showed that, *Obamacare is written to deceive.*

Point #4: *"Person"* has different Legal Definitions for different Purposes

So what else is Obamacare being deceptive about?

Well when Chief Justice Roberts referenced *Obamacare's* use of **"subchapter B of chapter 68"** he cited a statute from within that subchapter to support his interpretation of its usage — specifically, *§6671(a).*

If you look up *§6671(a),* you'll find that it does, indeed, support Robert's interpretation.

You also find, underneath it, *§6671(b)* — right where Chief Justice Roberts wanted you to find it.

Title 26, Chapter 68, Subchapter B, §6671(b) *states:*

• *The term "person", as used in this subchapter, includes an officer or employee of a corporation, or a member or employee of a partnership, who as such officer, employee, or member is under a duty to perform the act in respect of which the violation occurs.*

That's a *very* important definition of *"person."* But before we get into that subject — remember those other two enforcement tools that were supposedly banned from use but actually were not banned, discussed above in **Point #3**? The first was *criminal enforcement.* The second was *lien and levy powers.*

Criminal enforcement is found in **Chapter 75** of **Title 26**. Thus, the definition of *"person"* for the purposes of criminal enforcement is found in that chapter. Specifically, it is found in **Title 26, Chapter 75, §7343**, which reads:

• *The term "'person"' as used in this chapter includes an officer or employee of a corporation, or a member or employee of a partnership, who as such officer, employee, or member is under a duty to perform the act in respect of which the violation occurs.*

Finally, *lien and levy powers* are found in the *chapters* **63 and 64** specified by Chief Justice Roberts in his ruling where he references them as the *"assessment §6201(a)"* and *"collection §63013"* chapters, respectively. Now, *liens are only useful to enable levies,* so definitions for *levy powers* also reference *lien powers*. And in the **levy chapter (64)** at **§6332(f)** we find the following definition of *"person"*:

• *The term "person," as used in* **subsection (a)**, *includes an officer or employee of a corporation or a member or employee of a partnership, who as such officer, employee, or member is under a duty to surrender the property or rights to property, or to discharge the obligation.*

Take a moment at this point to compare *the three definitions of "person"* cited from references from Robert's ruling listed above that are found in *three different enforcement sections* of **Title 26**.

They are identical.

Yet, if you look up the *general* **Title 26** definition of *"person"* in **§7701(a)(1)** you'll find:

"The term "person" shall be construed to mean and include an individual, a trust, estate, partnership, association, company or corporation."

Notice that *generally speaking* for the entirety of **Title 26** the term *"person"* also means the term *'individual'*. That's why when the income tax laws and *Obamacare* laws address *'individuals' and 'persons'*, they have identical meanings.

But compare: the *general definition* of *"person"* in **§7701(a)(1)** above says it's just *"an individual, a trust, estate, partnership, association, company or corporation."* That's it, here, no fine print.

But the *definition of "person"* for *enforcement purposes* in the above cited **§§6671(b), 7343 and 6332(f)** are *way, way, more narrow.* To be that *'person',* you have to be: 1) *An officer or employee of a listed type of corporation;* AND 2) *Under a duty to perform an act;* AND 3) *In respect of said act, a violation occurs.*

That's a *lot* more specific than just being an *"individual, a trust, estate, partnership, association, company or corporation."*

So what does this difference in the three definitions of the term *"person"* mean? It means that the *definition of "person"* that the government can punish for tax violations, is NOT the same *definition of "person"* that is used in the rest of **Title 26**.

More specifically, it means that *the only "persons" that the government can impose tax violation enforcements against, are officers or employees of a corporation, who have a duty to act in some way regarding tax laws on behalf of their corporation, and who violate those tax laws on behalf of the corporation they officially represent.*

Do you represent a corporation in an official capacity to the government, on behalf of that corporation's tax obligations? If not, *then you are not a **§§6671(b), 7343 and 6332(f)** "person" who can be liable for violating the tax enforcement laws.*

And by direct reference through Obamacare itself, the enforcement laws that the government would use *to go after "persons"* it claims are violating Obamacare taxes OR penalties OR fines are *also found in **§§6671(b), 7343 and 6332(f)**.*

So *if you are not that definition of "person"*—which is repeated three different times in **Title 26** to make absolutely clear *exactly* who it is talking about—*then you are NOT liable for any other taxes which make use of the enforcement provisions linked to that definition, including income tax OR Obamacare.*

And in his ruling, Chief Justice Roberts *deliberately cited* a law which if you actually look it up is right next to the enforcement *definition of "person"* for **Chapter 68, Subchapter B**, *and he also indicated* that further enforcement definitions should be sought for the *fully applicable* criminal, and lien and levy chapters of **Title 26** — all of which turned out to be *identical enforcement definitions* for the term *"person".*

That extraordinary sequence of events is no accident — it is a *(whistleblower) communication.*

Point #5: *Taxpayers* are *Individuals* are *Persons*

So if the definition of *"person"* is so important, why do both the income tax laws and Obamacare laws refer to *"individuals"*?

To intentionally confuse you, of course! *And in any event they both refer to "taxpayers".*

Think of it this way – **Persons** or **individuals** may be subject to the enforcement of a particular tax, depending on a lot of things. **"Taxpayers"** however are *persons* or *individuals* who are subject to the enforcement of a particular tax.

That's why **Title 26, §7701(a)** states that *"The term taxpayer means any person subject to any internal revenue tax."*

So it's clear that both individuals and persons *may be subject to tax,* depending on *which* definitions of those terms apply to them.

IF they are *"liable",* THEN they are referred to as *"taxpayers."*

That's why *both* the income tax statutes and the *Obamacare* statutes make so much use of the term *"taxpayers".* When they are talking about someone who *might be subject to the tax,* then they use the terms *"person"* or *"individual".* But when they are talking about someone who *absolutely is subject to the tax,* then they use the term *"taxpayer."*

Point #6: *Imposed* Means *Enforced* – (Part 2)

Both the *income tax* and *Obamacare* start out by saying *"a tax is <u>imposed</u>".* Not *"a tax is made"* or a *"tax exists"* or just *"a tax".*

And <u>imposed</u> means *enforced.* If it can't be *enforced,* it can't be *imposed.*

So if it can't be <u>enforced</u> against *your definition of "person"* it can't be <u>imposed</u> on you.

Even (and especially) if you fit the *general* definition of *"person"* or *"individual"* but *not the enforcement definition of "person".*

And if it can't be <u>imposed</u> on you, *you can't be a*

taxpayer for it.

And if you're not a *taxpayer* for it… *it doesn't apply to you.*

Point #7: News Flash – The Chief Justice of the United States Supreme Court *Knows All of This*

But if he knows it, then why didn't he say it?

Well he <u>did</u> say it. Specifically, Roberts wrote, *"The Federal Government does not have the power <u>to order people</u> to buy health insurance. **Section 5000A** would therefore be <u>unconstitutional</u> if read <u>as a command</u>. The Federal Government does have the power to impose a tax on <u>those</u> without health insurance. **Section 5000A** is therefore <u>constitutional</u>, because it can reasonably be read <u>as a tax</u>."*

Did you catch it?

This is the paragraph that drives everyone crazy. This is the paragraph that makes everyone scream that Roberts is crazy. But apply what has been explained above to what Roberts wrote. He's talking about what *"The Federal Government"* has *"the power"* to do. And as has been explained you have to ask yourself: *do what to whom?*

He says: *"the power to <u>order people</u> to buy"*. Then he says: *"the power to <u>impose a tax</u> on <u>those</u>"*.

He's differentiating! *"<u>People</u>"* are not the same as *"<u>those!</u>"*

Order people — the government does NOT have the power to "order" a free people...to do anything.

Impose tax on those — the government DOES have the power to "*impose*" on "*those*" because "*THOSE*" are TAXPAYERS!

Taxpayers are - *literally by triple definition* - *imposed persons* subject to enforcement via the detailed descriptions provided in *§§ 6671(b), 7343* and *6332(f)* of *Title 26*, specifically 1) *an officer or employee of a listed type of corporation,* AND 2) *under a duty to perform an act,* AND 3) *in respect of said act a violation occurs.*

And regarding "*those persons*"—and ONLY "*those persons*"—Chief Justice Roberts ruled that *Obamacare* IS Constitutional:

"*The Federal Government DOES have the power to impose a tax on those without health insurance.*"

HOWEVER, he also specifically ruled that *against the people* — as in We The People — *Obamacare is NOT constitutional:*

"*The Federal Government does not have the power to order people to buy health insurance.*"

Roberts *specifically protected the constitutional freedom of the American People,* right in front of their eyes, according to the *actual meaning* of the *tax laws...* *...after ruling against any other constitutional clause that could serve to confuse the tax issues.*

And *THIS* is the reason why no other Justice would support him — *because in doing so, Roberts Isolated and Exposed* <u>The Government's Secret of LIMITED TAX LIABILITY</u>!

Point #8: The Two Powers

If you've come this far and didn't know this material beforehand you might be in a bit of a shock at this point. Basically the reason that <u>*Obamacare doesn't apply to 95% of Americans*</u> is because <u>*Obamacare can only be enforced against people responsible for running corporations*</u> – not normal people simply working and living on their own personal behalf. And more, *those limitations on the enforcement laws don't come out of Obamacare;* rather, *they're a part of the income tax laws that have been there all along,* that *Obamacare* has attached itself to in order to make use of them.

Can this really be possible? It means that <u>*there are two separate enforcement powers*</u> *held by the Federal government* – one for <u>*corporation persons*</u> and one for *regular human-being-type,* <u>*non-corporate natural persons*</u>. And that <u>*a giant scam*</u> has taken place by the government using <u>*legally defined terms*</u> such as *"person,"* and *"individual",* and *"taxpayer",* in order to confuse these identities and especially <u>*to hide the two different powers of government. And the government's fraud against the people*</u>.

Well, let's look at Chief Justice Roberts again and see what he said about this subject. In his ruling, Roberts wrote:

"This case concerns two powers that the Constitution does grant the Federal Government, but which must be read carefully to avoid creating a general federal authority akin to the police power."

Now that's a hell of a thing to say isn't it? *"This case concerns two powers."* If you disregard the analysis presented above, ask yourself — *what two powers?*

After all isn't that why the country has been ripping itself to shreds over Robert's ruling—because it's only taking into account a single power—that of the Federal government? You might say, Well, there's the powers of the *Commerce clause* and the *Necessary and Proper clause* that Roberts threw out when he kept the *Taxing power* in. But that's *three powers,* total, *not two.* So what's the difference between them? *How do you turn three powers into two?* And for that matter, why should there be multiple powers in the first place? *Don't we have only one government?*

No we don't. We have *two governments* in fact. *Two completely separate governments* under one Constitution.

The first government is the original one. *It deals with human beings* acting as human beings and nothing else. That government has to deal with a position derived from those human beings. And those human beings are acknowledged as possessing God-given natural rights, that existed *before the "government" was created,* and which cannot be removed by *that "government"* because it simply does not have the authority to do so.

The second government however is exactly the opposite of the first one. *The second government creates, controls and runs corporations.* The very word *"incorporate"* means *"give body to"* or *"bring into existence."* And because *that "government"* creates corporations, it *owns those corporation completely — because of the fact that it is their creator.*

Thus legally, *corporations are slaves to the "government" that created them,* by definition. They are created, live in obedience to, and die at the command of *that "government"* — including *paying taxes* to *that "government."* And the rules that *that "government"* can make for those corporations are *literally unlimited,* because *those corporations have no rights.* They only have *privileges* that are granted to them by their *creator "government",* privileges which can be changed or terminated at any time, solely at the pleasure of *that "government."*

Functionally, *those are the* two governments which comprise the two *main Federal jurisdictional powers* of our *one constitutional Republic.* And thusly, *they are the two powers* to which Roberts is referring. And he acknowledges them *both* as constitutionally legitimate.

But he also warns that *it is extremely dangerous* to mix them up. In fact, he points out that *if you mix them up, you can end up with* what he calls *"a general federal authority akin to the police power."*

But isn't that exactly what everyone is afraid Roberts has actually done with his ruling?

Yet *here* he is specifically *warning everyone* against making that interpretation of his ruling, and teaching that the way to avoid that terrible mistake is to *"read carefully."*

So that's what this analysis is — a very, very careful reading. It is not *my interpretation* of Roberts. It is my careful *reading* of what *Roberts actually said* per his specific instructions.

Two governmental powers exist. Roberts said so and warned against confusing them. For the Chief Justice said that *if we mix them up WE will create by our very ignorance "a general federal authority akin to the police power."*

So what does this mean? It means *enabling* the Federal government *through Obamacare* to start treating *We The People* of *inalienable human rights* like wholly-owned government-privileged *corporations* for *everything.*

Point #9: *Bait and Switch* and *Presumption*

But wait a second (I imagine you say again). What about forcing everyone to pay income tax *already?* If *Obamacare* doesn't apply to 95% of Americans because it is imposed by corporate income tax enforcement laws, *then how the hell does the government get away with applying those same corporate income tax enforcement laws to non-corporate, regular human people-persons for the income tax?*

Ans: *You volunteer to be treated as a corporation.*

Remember in his ruling that Roberts said that *"without a careful reading"* you can create *"a general federal authority akin to the police power"* concerning Obamacare? *And the income tax too.*

Well concerning the income tax, *most Americans have NOT made a "careful reading" of the tax laws and HAVE THEMSELVES*, therefore, created a *"federal authority akin to the police power"* concerning the subject of *individual income taxes.*

You see, as free human beings, *we have the right to make contracts.* And there is such a thing as a *government presumed contract.* What the government has done is *argued to the courts* – and the courts have unlawfully agreed – *that the government is not responsible for people's legal ignorance,* and that if they act in such a way as to *functionally volunteer to be treated as a corporation,* then the government gets to treat them like *a corporation.* Even worse, courts have fraudulently agreed that *neither they, nor other government officials, have to tell you that you're being treated as a corporation* under the interpretation that *you don't need to be told* since you *supposedly volunteered* in the first place. (*Non-disclosure is a fraud*).

And then, to top it off, the government has created rules to make it extremely difficult, if not impossible, *for you to NOT be treated like a corporation anymore,* by presuming that until you have *proven that you are not a corporation,* they get to pound you just as if you were a corporation that was *faking being a human being.* As a result you can actually be convicted for fraud and go to jail for demanding that you *not* be treated as if you were a corporation!

That's the way it is; that's the fraud.

So the *technical answer* is *No, 95% of Americans don't have to pay the income tax* because it's enforcement mechanisms specify that <u>*only corporations or people responsible for corporations*</u> are subject to income tax enforcement.

The *practical answer,* however, is that without a *lot* of money and legal representation, the government will use *their presumption* that you *are* a corporation against you to seize your money and property, and throw you in jail, *long* before you can get through all the court hearings necessary for them to admit that <u>*you are a non-corporate human being-type person*</u>. Or they will simply show you that *that's what they are going to do to you,* unless you sign a document agreeing that you *are in fact* a corporation, *and* agree that you've been a *very, very bad corporation* and that you deserve to pay all sorts of fines in order to stay out of jail.

That's the way it is; that's the fraud.

So DO NOT THINK you can use the information in this analysis—even by quoting Chief Justice John Roberts of the United States Supreme Court—to stop paying income taxes.

It Won't Work; that's the fraud.

The IRS will simply STOMP you into oblivion, because

24

legally, *they get to treat you under the presumption* that you *are* a corporation—*and they don't have to acknowledge any "presumed corporations" that try to claim they are not corporations.*

In fact, the *technical legal name* for that particular argument is *"frivolous."*

That's right, according to tax laws, interpretations and rulings *pointing out that you are a human being who does not fit the specifications of the actual income tax enforcement laws — is frivolous.*

Not *"funny-frivolous."*

But rather, *"go-to-jail-frivolous."*

Read carefully: you are warned.

Point #10: Generalization – A Bridge Too Far!

Contrary to what most people think, *judges can't just go rule on something if they think it is wrong.* They have to wait for *an appropriate case* to come to them, and sometimes it never does. Also, cases themselves have all sorts of issues and parts to them. Sometimes a case will seem to be about one thing, but it's actually about another. So for the purposes of *what it seems to be about,* it's useless. And if *political operatives* have decided that certain types of cases will be ruled *against their interests* by certain judges, every effort will be made by those *political operatives* to keep those cases *out of those courts.* Thus a judge can wait a whole career and never rule on what he or she wants to rule on.

The opposite is also true. Sometimes a case show up, and a judge realizes – *this is it; now or never;* another opportunity may never come, or come too late to matter. *So they act.*

This I believe is what Chief Justice Roberts has done with his *Obamacare Ruling.* If he waited longer to make this ruling, Obamacare would be in another form and perhaps not so amenable to exposure for what it really is. Or such a vast bureaucracy will have been formed by the time he got to rule on it that enormous damage to the country would have been done in the mean time. Or he simply might not have gotten to be the swing vote and would have been out-voted no matter what his position was.

So he chose this; and he chose Now.

But what did he actually do?

Simply put, *he raised the alarm* about something that goes far, far beyond Obamacare. In fact *it goes straight to the heart of why everyone is so upset.* Roberts not only drew attention to the fact that *by simply positioning anything they want as a tax the government can force anyone to do anything at any time, he certified that concept as constitutional.* And by doing that, he made sure that the vulnerability of the country to totally legal tyranny would never go away. For even if Obamacare was repealed, *his ruling would still stand,* and Congress could just try again later with something else.

But why would Roberts do such a thing? After all, he warned against the creation of *"a general federal authority akin to the police power."* And he also said elsewhere in his ruling that *"our respect for Congress's policy judgments thus can never extend so far as to disavow restraints on federal power that the Constitution carefully constructed."* Yet after saying these things, _he then went and enabled them!_

Except he didn't. Because he pointed out – *subtly, but clearly, for those who follow his hints as I have here –* that _these powers Congress is trying to use against the People do not in fact apply to them but only to Corporations_ !

But the man is a Federal Judge – the TOP Federal Judge. Do you think Roberts isn't fully aware of what the IRS "legally" does to people who try to use *Roberts own argument* against the IRS?

Of course he does.

That's why he wrote the argument. Because now, *HE WRITE THIS ARGUMENT*—not *YOU.*

And *this matters,* because *by definition,* the Chief Justice of the United States Supreme Court *is not frivolous. Even by the interpretations of the IRS.*

You see, *Roberts jammed the machine*. And scared the *crap* out of the entire Federal government by doing it. *That's* why no other Justice would join him—*he terrified them too*.

And he did it because it was the only way he could find to **halt** the *unstoppable expansion of a process* that was *originally promised by Congress to be limited only to the income tax* – but technically could be applied to *anything at all Congress wanted.*

What was that process?

• The Federal government's ability to *presume that natural human person Americans had volunteered to be treated as corporations under the law;*

• The Federal government's ability to do this *without telling the people* that such *a presumption* had been made against them;

• The Federal government's ability to *use* this presumption *to deny Americans* their inalienable constitutional rights by *replacing them with government-controlled corporate privileges;*

• And finally, The Federal government's ability to *not tell Americans how to get out of that presumption* without being harmed by trying to do so.

When Obamacare came up as a tax law Roberts – *and all the Justices* – knew what this meant. It meant that Congress had *gone back on* their promise to presume this terrible corporate tax power upon people *only for the purpose of the income tax,* and now use it for *everything* because *Obamacare* is the *generalization of this principle that opens the door to its infinite use.* As long as the *only application* of these tax laws were for income taxes, that single application stood as a kind of limitation. But *with a second application* the principle becomes *generalized,* and with that the door swings open wide.

But the *real problem* is that it is legal. Yet Roberts did not make it legal – it was made legal long before Roberts was born. *People have a constitutional right to contract, and contracts can be presumed by behavior.* And *ignorance of the law is not an excuse.* It's all there—*in its application to tax laws*—and now *Obamacare* (*and with that literally everything else*) its *unconcienableness* has become *diabolical !*

So what was Roberts to do? Throw it out? If he did that, it would come back. Obama's administration is obviously licking it's chops over expanding this principle of *empowerment through tax enforcement. Obamacare,* or something like it, or something else, would come back again, and again, and again – and each time *it would be technically constitutional.*

So Roberts decided to take a conscientious stand. Like John Hancock, signing his name big enough on the Declaration of Independence to make sure the King saw it, *Chief Justice Roberts ensured,* with the signing of his Obamacare Ruling, *that unless everyone works together no one is ever going home to freedom again.* Because *the only way out of this problem is for Americans to know about it, understand it, and enforce the constitutional protection against it.*

By separating the Executive and Judicial powers.

Not against corporations, per se. But against people being treated as corporations and losing their rights through presumption.

Remember Pelosi gloating that you'd have to pass Obamacare to see what was in it? She was telling you the truth about the government's use of presumption. The government presumes that you have voluntarily surrendered your humanity for corporate status, and then passes bills without telling you what's in them, *because you have no right to know what your corporate masters are doing until they want to tell you.* Even then they don't have to tell you – Pelosi didn't say she'd explain it, just that you could read it if it was passed.

That's what happens if you fight the IRS too – *the IRS is allowed to presume that the corporate laws apply to you,* and that you therefore have to pay the tax before you can challenge the tax in court. But then, if you pay and fight, *the government doesn't have to tell you that you're being treated as a volunteer corporation.* Instead, they rule that *your claims of humanity are frivolous because you're obeying corporate laws and standing in a corporate administrative court.* This secret presumption has been repeatedly misruled as being Constitutional. You just didn't know about it.

So you can see why those who would convert the *entirety* of the Constitution into tax laws, are *drunk on the mechanism of presumption.* That's why Pelosi replied, when asked if Obamacare was Constitutional, "Are you serious!?? Are you serious!??" *Look at her reply legally:* she mocked the question as *frivolous.* In doing so she limited her response to *only incorporated* "persons"!

And remember, she was saying this as *Speaker of the House of Representatives.* In other words, she wasn't without authority when she said it. She specifically invoked *the power of secret presumption* by using contempt in order to *hide behind* its legal protections. Government employees use this *indemnification technique* all the time, *because the people don't know it's a legal statement !*

Before Obamacare, secret presumption mean income tax. Now, it means people forced to face death panels and perform abortions against their religious beliefs – when they don't actually have to!

That's why *SECRET PRESUMPTION is the monumental problem* Roberts has chosen to expose with his courageous ruling. And he did it now because our country is poised on the edge of a precipice — right now. Compared to the absolute catastrophe of generalizing the secret taxing authority presumption, all the hell of *Obamacare* is merely one example with an infinite number of the same kinds of tax laws right behind it waiting only for Congress to vote.

But Roberts showed the SOLUTION to the problem when he wrote that "The Framers created a Federal Government of limited powers, and assigned to this Court the duty of enforcing those limits.

But the Court does not express any opinion on the wisdom of the Affordable Care Act (*Obamacare). Under the Constitution, that judgment is reserved to the People."*

Only *the People* can put a *Constitutional Stop* to the government's *currently LEGAL but fraudulent use of* <u>*the secret presumption of corporate status*</u> against human beings. *Robert's can't do that himself.* But in a single astonishing ruling, Chief Justice Roberts *has warned the American People of what is being done to them, how it is being done, and the* <u>*immanent danger*</u> *of its expansion of use.*

What the American People *will now do* about this problem remains to be seen. One thing is sure, though, — the more people who know about it, the better.

<u>*Peaceful change can only come from knowledge.*</u> <u>*So pass on the word.*</u>

END OF ARTICLE

So is Justice Roberts a traitor? Or is he a real American hero? I say it all depends on whether or not we the people pay attention to what he has done and act accordingly. It seems to me that it is abundantly clear that now more than ever before in the history of this country *it is imperative that we do NOT comply!*

Do as you wish, of course, but be prepared to suffer the consequences of the actions you have been manipulated into taking in order to justify the consequences.

Many of you out there know who Chaplain Lindsay Williams is and have probably heard his interviews over the past few years, but his latest one involves information about just exactly what the *Affordable Care Act* really is and just exactly why it was shoved down our throats. At the very least you had better listen to what he has to say about those *Smart Meters* and get busy getting rid of, or neutralizing yours. (*See, December 4, 2013*).

http://radio.goldseek.com/nuggets.php

Yes, America, for the sake of all humanity we must *See Something and Say something* loud and annoyingly repetitive because...

WE ARE THE ANSWER!!!

Video Starring Liars, Cheats, Criminals (Congress) Traitors; and maybe *One more Patriot — YOU!*

IT ALL DEPENDS ON YOU!

Chief Justice John Roberts is an American Hero!

Chief Justice John Roberts recently ruled that Obamacare is Constitutional as a tax and that *Obamacare penalties are part of the income tax return, therefore, Obamacare does NOT apply to 95% of the American population!*

Obamacare is "written to deceive" so Roberts warned Americans to read carefully his ruling dealing with this law that is written to deceive.

What is *Obamacare* being deceptive about? The *definitions of the "person"* that the government can punish for tax violations.

More specifically, the only *"persons"* that the government can impose tax violation enforcements against are *"officers or employees of a corporation, who have a duty to act in some way regarding tax laws on behalf of their corporation, and who violate those tax laws on behalf of the corporation they officially represent."*

Therefore, if you do not represent a corporation in an official capacity to the government on behalf of that corporation's tax obligations, then you are not a *"person"* who can be liable for violating the tax enforcement laws.

You are not liable for any other taxes which make use of the enforcement provisions linked with *Obamacare,* including the individual income tax.

Hence Robert's whistleblower communication.

Both the *income tax laws* and *Obamacare laws* refer to *"individuals"* to intentionally confuse you of course since both laws refer to *"taxpayers".*

"Taxpayers" are *persons* or *individuals* subject to the enforcement of a particular tax.

When officials are talking about someone *who is subject to a tax* they use the term *"taxpayer"* but when they are talking about someone who *might be subject to a tax* they use the term *"individual"*.

Roberts specifically wrote that *"The federal government does not have the power to order people to buy health insurance."*

Roberts also wrote that *"The Federal Government does have the power to impose a tax on those without health insurance".*

See the dichotomy here? The contrast between two things that are entirely different!

He's talking here about what the Federal Government has *"the power to do"*. *"The power to order people to buy"* and *"the power to impose a tax on those".*

"Order people" — the government *does not* have the power to "order" a free people to do anything.

"Impose a tax on those" — the government *does* have the power to "impose" a tax on "those" because "those" are "taxpayers".

Against the "people" Obamacare IS NOT constitutional

Against "taxpayers" Obamacare IS constitutional

Obamacare can only be enforced against people who are responsible for running corporations; not against normal people simply working and living on their own behalf.

These limitations on the enforcement law are part of the income tax laws that have been there all along.

Roberts' Ruling Isolated and Exposed the Federal Government's secret of *LIMITED TAX LIABILITY* and the two separate enforcement powers that the Federal Government has — *one for corporation "persons"* and *one* for _natural "persons"_ — and the <u>_Giant Scam_</u> that has taken place by the Federal Government to hide its two powers of government.

Roberts writes that _"This case concerns two powers that the Constitution does grant the Federal Government, but which must be read carefully to avoid creating a general federal authority akin to the police power"._

In other words, _Obamacare concerns two powers._

What two powers?

We have two separate _"governments"_ under one Constitution.

The first _"government"_ deals with _human beings._ The second _"government"_ deals with and controls _Corporations._

Corporations are slaves to the _"government"_ that created them.

Those two _"governments"_ comprise the two Federal Jurisdictional powers of our one Constitutional Republic. And both are constitutionally legitimate.

But we've mixed them up and created _"a general federal authority akin to the police power"._

Two governmental powers exist and we've mixed them up and created, by our very ignorance, _"a general federal authority akin to the police power"_ enabling the Federal Government to treat us, _the natural people,_ like wholly owned government-privileged Corporations, through the bait and switch of the principle of _"presumption"._

By _"presumption"_ the Federal Government has applied those same corporate income tax enforcement laws to non-corporate human beings for the individual income tax.

The Federal Government _"presumes"_ that you have _volunteered_ to be treated as a corporation.

Roberts is saying that *"without a careful reading"* of corporate income tax enforcement laws, we have created a *"federal authority akin to the police power"* concerning the individual income tax by *volunteering* to be treated as a corporation.

The Collusion of Executive and Judicial branches

Knowing that we have the right to make contracts and that there is such a thing as a presumed contract, the government and the courts *colluded* to agree that the government is not responsible for the people's legal ignorance, and that if the people act in such a way as to functionally volunteer to be treated as a corporation, then the government gets to treat them like a corporation.

Even worse, courts have fraudulently agreed that neither they nor other government officials have to tell you that you're being treated as a corporation, under the interpretation that you don't need to be told because you volunteered to be treated as a corporation in the first place.

Moreover, the government has created rules to make it difficult, if not impossible, for you to NOT be treated like a corporation, by presuming that until you *prove to the government* that you are not a corporation, they get to pound you down as a corporation *faking to be human.*

Claiming that you are a human being does not fit the specifications of the income tax enforcement laws, so your viewpoint is deemed to be frivolous.

Roberts' Ruling on Obamacare

So Roberts has raised the alarm!

Roberts not only drew attention to the fact that by simply positioning anything they want as a tax, the government can force anyone to do anything at any time that they want. He certified this concept as constitutional making sure that the *vulnerability of the United States to total legal tyranny* would never go away. For even if Obamacare were repealed, Robert's Ruling would still stand and Congress could try again later with something else.

Yet after saying these things, Roberts pointed out, subtly but clearly, that the powers that Congress is trying to use against the People, do not in fact apply to them but only to Corporations!

And Roberts is a Federal Judge — the TOP Federal Judge, and by definition, the rulings of The Chief Justice of the United States Supreme Court are not frivolous even by the interpretations of the IRS.

Roberts jammed the machine as the only way to stop the *collusion* that was originally promised by Congress to the Judiciary in 1933, to limit the process to the income tax, though technically it could be applied to anything Congress ever wanted to do. Meaning:

• The Federal government's ability to *presume that natural-human-person Americans have volunteered to be treated as corporations under the law;*

• The Federal government's ability to do this *without telling the people* that such *a presumption* has been made against them;

• The Federal government's ability to *use* this presumption *to deny Americans* their inalienable constitutional rights by *replacing them* with government-controlled *corporate privileges;*

• The Federal government's ability to *not tell Americans how to get out of that presumption without being harmed by trying to do so.*

The introduction of Obamacare as a tax law meant that Congress had gone back on their 1933 promise to the Judiciary to *presume* this *terrible corporate tax power* upon people only for the purpose of the income tax and not use it for anything else.

Obamacare is a generalization of the principle of *empowerment through tax enforcement* that opens the door to its infinite use.

People have a constitutional right to contract, and contracts can be presumed by behavior - and ignorance of the law is not an excuse. But the application of this principle to to tax laws, and now to Obamacare, is diabolical!

Roberts took a conscientious stand to ensure that everyone would work together, or they never would be free.

The only way out of this problem is for Americans to know about it, understand it, and enforce the constitutional protection against it — the *separation* of the Executive and Judicial powers as they were constitutionally designed to be.

Before Obamacare, secret presumption applied to the collection of income tax. Now it means people forced to face death panels and perform abortions against their religious beliefs — when they don't actually have to!

SECRET PRESUMPTION is the monumental problem *Roberts chose to expose with his courageous ruling.* And he exposed it now because our country is poised on the edge of a precipice.

Roberts showed the SOLUTION to the problem when he wrote that, *"The Framers created a Government of limited* *powers, and assigned to this Court the duty of enforcing those* *limits. But the Court does not express any opinion on the* *wisdom of the Affordable Care Act (i.e., Obamacare). Under* *the Constitution, that judgment is reserved to the People."*

Only the People can put a Constitutional Stop to the government's currently *LEGAL* but *FRAUDILENT* use of *the* *secret presumption of corporate status* against human beings.

Robert's can't do that himself, but in his single astonishing ruling, Chief Justice Roberts told the American People *what is being done to them, how it is being done to them, and the immanent danger of its expansion of use.*

What the American People will now do about this problem remains to be seen. One thing is sure, though, — the more people who know about it the better.

Peaceful change can only come from knowledge. So pass this word around.

Justice Roberts is a real American hero! That is abundantly clear now more than ever before in the history of these United States!

Congress Colludes with the Courts:

The Government and the Courts UNCONSTITUTIONALLY agreed that the Government doesn't have to acknowledge any *presumed corporation* that tries to claim that they are *NOT a corporation.* The Government promised the Courts to limit the *process of presumption* presuming that natural person Americans have *volunteered to be treated as corporation* under the law, to the income tax return.

Congress Colludes with the Banks:

The Government and the Banks UNCONSTITUTIONALLY agreed to allow the Banks to treat their Depositors as Corporations printed in all-capital-letter names on their checks that the Makers sign as *Representative* on the *micro-print signature line* (MP) that repeats over and over again *"authorized representative, authorized representative, authorized representative"...* to conform with the fact that the only *"persons"* that the government can impose tax violation enforcements against are *"officers or employees of a corporation, who have a duty to act in some way regarding tax laws on behalf of their corporation, and who violate those tax laws on behalf of the corporation they officially represent."*

Therefore, according to the unconstitutional Government, Courts and the Banks, *you represent* a Corporation *in an official capacity to the government on behalf of that corporation's tax obligations,* so you are presumed by them to be a *"person"* who can be liable for violating the tax enforcement laws — *unless, you Object!*

http://Maine-Patriot.com